Shake, F~~~
and Roll

Contents

Hot Rocks	4
Crash Course	6
On Shaky Ground	8
Living on a Fault Line	10
Wall of Water	12
What a Blast!	14
Inside a Volcano	15
Ring of Fire	18
Rivers of Lava	20
Gas and Ash	22
After an Eruption	24
Keeping Watch	26
Staying Safe	28
Glossary	30
Index	31
Research Starters	32

Features

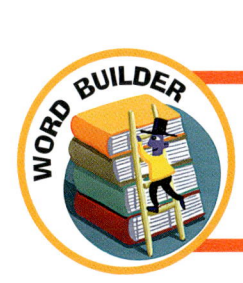

WORD BUILDER

Do you know there is a place called Vulcano? Why do you think it has that name? Find out more on page 16.

FAST FACTS

Volcanoes can be very destructive. Read about the damage caused by a very active volcano in Hawaii on page 21.

IN THE NEWS

Find out what happened when a volcano erupted near the city of Quito in Ecuador. Take a look at **Ash Chokes City** on page 23.

IN FOCUS

Do you live in an earthquake area? Find out if you are prepared in **Are You Earthquake-Ready?** on page 29.

SITESEEING • PAST & FUTURE

What was found at Pompeii?

Visit **www.infosteps.co.uk**
for more about POMPEII.

Hot Rocks

Over 6,000 kilometres beneath Earth's surface is a deep fiery centre or core. Temperatures are over fifty times hotter than boiling water. Surrounding the core is the mantle, a 2,900-kilometre thick layer of explosive hot rock and metal. The thin rocky shell surrounding the mantle is known as the crust.

The fierce heat and pressure deep below the surface generates earthquakes and volcanoes. Earth's surface is constantly changing due to the shake, rumble and roll of Earth's fiery core.

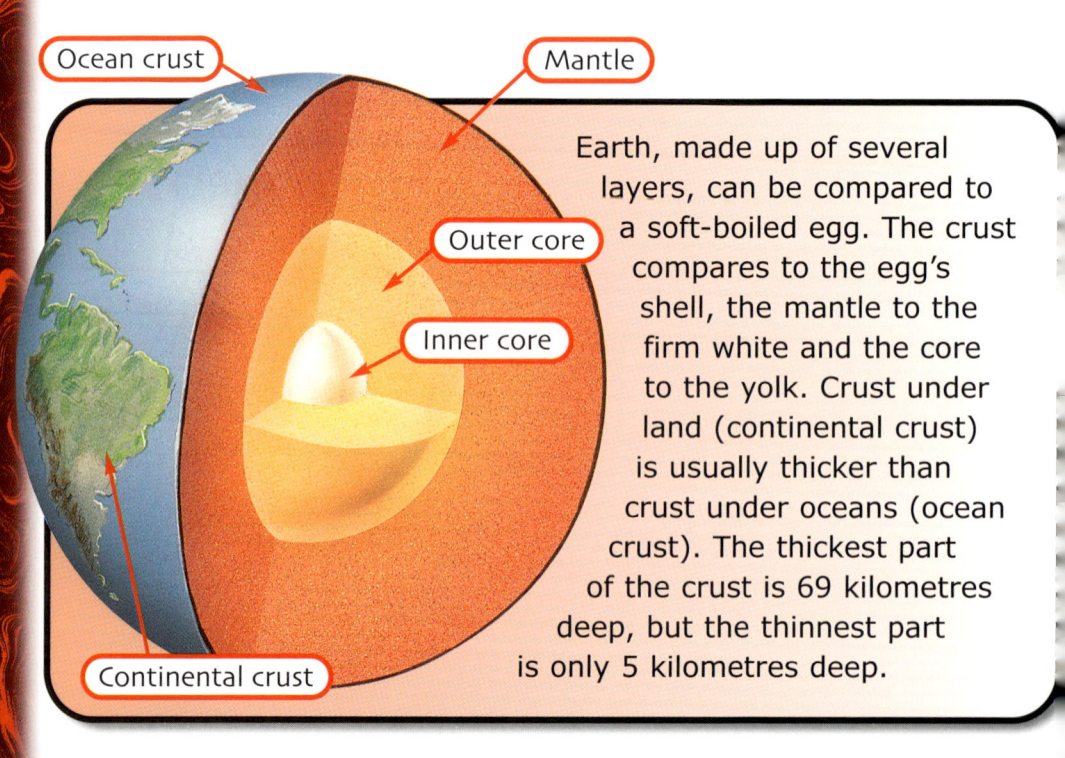

Ocean crust
Mantle
Outer core
Inner core
Continental crust

Earth, made up of several layers, can be compared to a soft-boiled egg. The crust compares to the egg's shell, the mantle to the firm white and the core to the yolk. Crust under land (continental crust) is usually thicker than crust under oceans (ocean crust). The thickest part of the crust is 69 kilometres deep, but the thinnest part is only 5 kilometres deep.

No Short Cuts!

If you could drill a tunnel from your home through the centre of Earth to the other side where would you end up?

You would probably need a lifetime to drill through the nearly 13,000 kilometres from one side of Earth to the other. By the time the toughest drill had reached only 13 kilometres below the surface, however, it would have melted from the extreme heat.

Crash Course

Earth's crust and an upper layer of the mantle are made up of ten huge rocky plates and about twenty smaller ones. The heat in Earth's core creates strong **convection currents** that push the plates in different directions. Although you can't feel it these plates are constantly moving, shifting and shaping the surface of Earth.

Earth's plates are constantly moving. The arrows show the direction of movement.

▲ Volcanoes

Earthquake zones

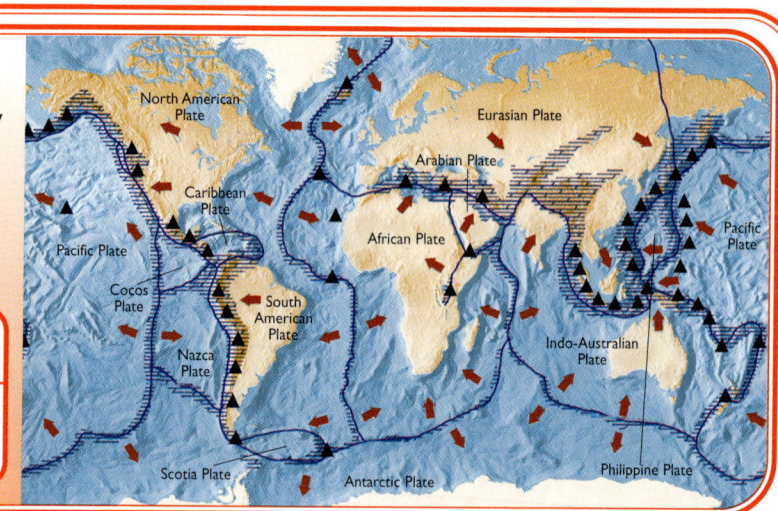

Many scientists believe Earth's land was one huge continent about 200 million years ago. Over millions of years the continent split into smaller land masses. The movement of the plates has joined and divided the land masses.

200 million years ago

90 million years ago

Present

Predicted in 60 million year's time

Crashing plates cause earthquakes and create mountain ranges and volcanoes. When India hit Eurasia 60 million years ago the highest mountains on Earth, the Himalayas, were formed.

Heat causes Earth's plates to crash, separate and slide past each other.

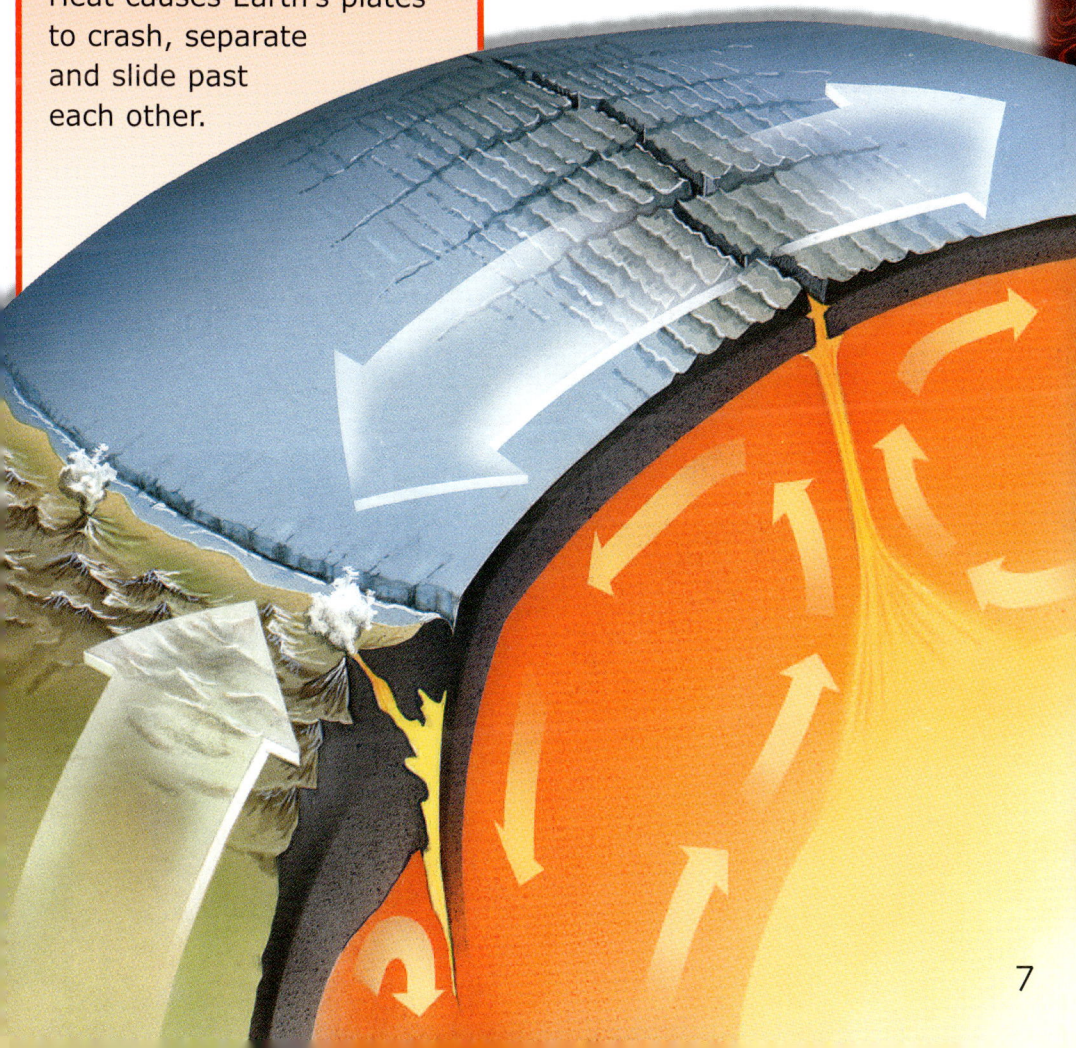

On Shaky Ground

Have you ever felt the ground shake? If you have you may have been feeling an earthquake. Small earthquakes can cause objects to fall from shelves. Large earthquakes can cause windows to shatter, buildings and bridges to collapse and roads and railway tracks to bend and break. They can also cause landslides, flooding and fire.

Earth shakes slightly every thirty seconds, but these **tremors** are too small to be felt. Around forty earthquakes that are large enough to cause damage happen each year. A major earthquake usually occurs somewhere in the world about every two or three years.

In 1995 a devastating earthquake destroyed the city of Kobe, Japan. Highways collapsed and railway lines bulged. Fires caused by broken gas pipes swept through the city. Firefighters were unable to stop the spreading fires because the water pipes had also broken.

Searching for survivors is an important job after an earthquake. Sniffer dogs that are trained to find people are often sent into collapsed buildings.

Living on a Fault Line

Many earthquakes occur along a **fault**, where sections of Earth's rocky outer crust are constantly sliding past each other. The **friction** between the two plates creates earthquakes. Most faults lie deep beneath Earth's surface. Some, however, such as the San Andreas Fault in the US state of California, can be clearly seen from an aeroplane.

There are tiny tremors every day in California and nearly every year a destructive earthquake occurs somewhere within the state. Most of these earthquakes and tremors are caused by movement along the San Andreas Fault.

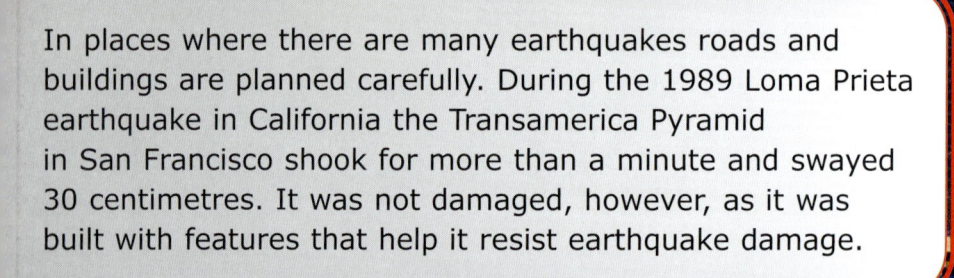

In places where there are many earthquakes roads and buildings are planned carefully. During the 1989 Loma Prieta earthquake in California the Transamerica Pyramid in San Francisco shook for more than a minute and swayed 30 centimetres. It was not damaged, however, as it was built with features that help it resist earthquake damage.

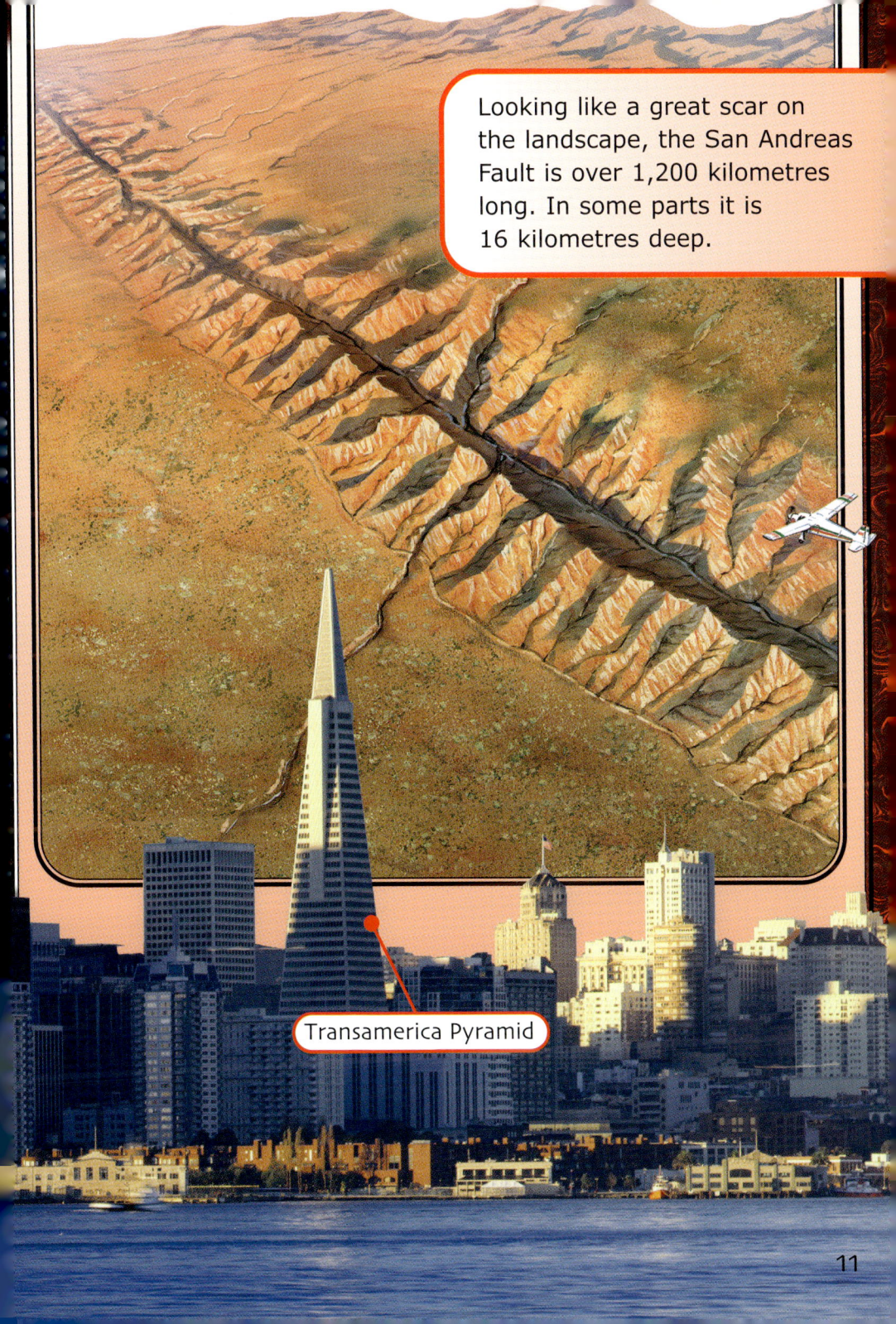

Looking like a great scar on the landscape, the San Andreas Fault is over 1,200 kilometres long. In some parts it is 16 kilometres deep.

Transamerica Pyramid

Wall of Water

A tsunami, tidal wave or tidal surge is a towering ocean wave which can be caused by a jolt to the ocean floor from an earthquake, landslide or volcanic eruption. The giant wave speeds across the ocean before crashing onto land. It causes little disturbance until it meets shallow water, where the wave reaches its greatest height.

Scientists use special equipment to find out when a tsunami will happen. They then measure the speed at which the tsunami is travelling. People who are in danger can be warned and given time to get to a safe place.

Because a tsunami starts far out at sea people on shore cannot see it building.

As a tsunami comes closer to land it can suck the water from a harbour. People should leave the area quickly.

When a tsunami hits land any buildings or people in its path are swept far out to sea.

Inside a Volcano

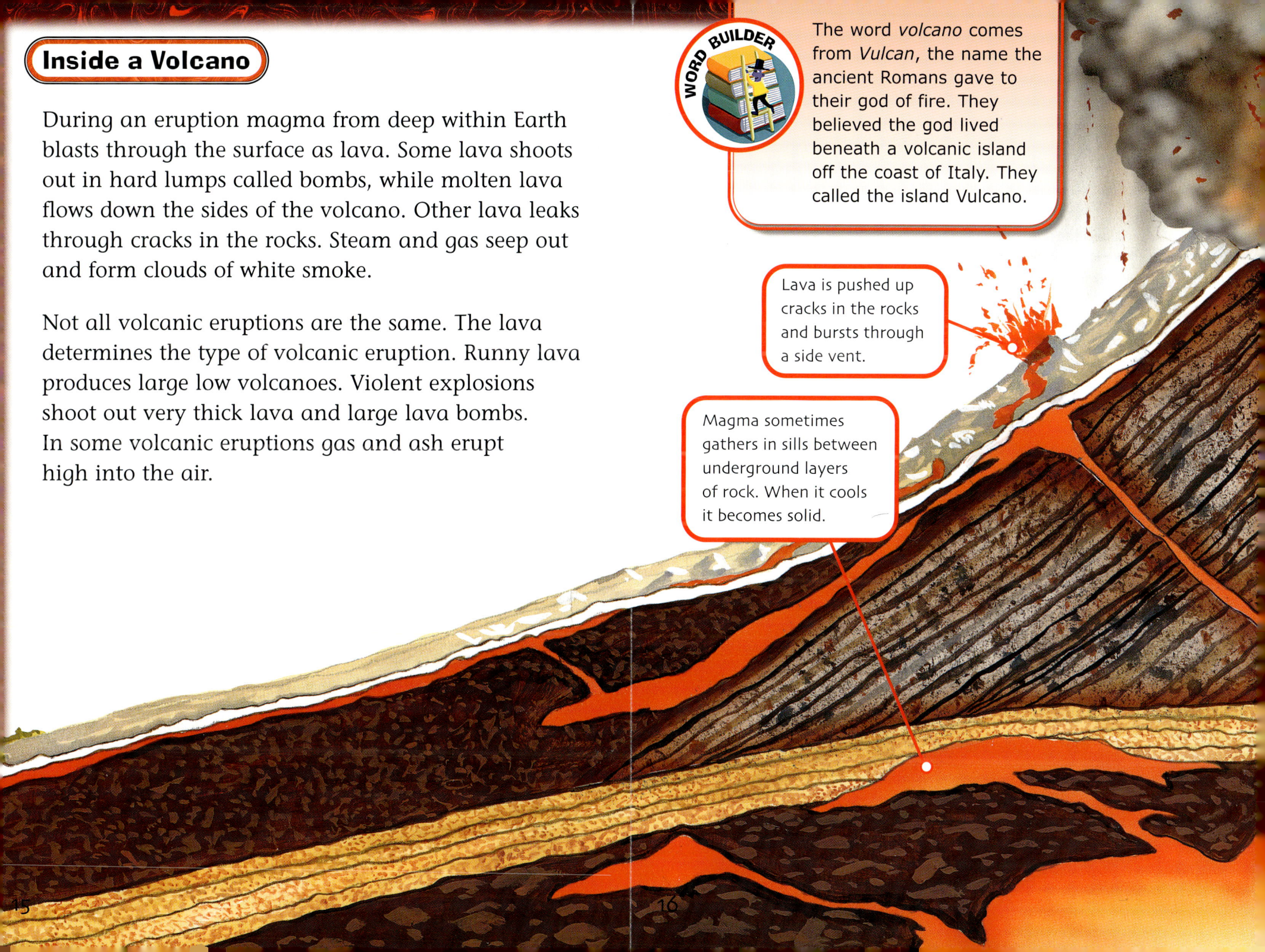

During an eruption magma from deep within Earth blasts through the surface as lava. Some lava shoots out in hard lumps called bombs, while molten lava flows down the sides of the volcano. Other lava leaks through cracks in the rocks. Steam and gas seep out and form clouds of white smoke.

Not all volcanic eruptions are the same. The lava determines the type of volcanic eruption. Runny lava produces large low volcanoes. Violent explosions shoot out very thick lava and large lava bombs. In some volcanic eruptions gas and ash erupt high into the air.

WORD BUILDER

The word *volcano* comes from *Vulcan*, the name the ancient Romans gave to their god of fire. They believed the god lived beneath a volcanic island off the coast of Italy. They called the island Vulcano.

Lava is pushed up cracks in the rocks and bursts through a side vent.

Magma sometimes gathers in sills between underground layers of rock. When it cools it becomes solid.

What a Blast! continued

Ring of Fire

When two plates collide one may slowly slide under the other. This is called **subduction**. Deep below the crust rocks in the lower plate melt and rise close to the surface. The melted rock, or magma, may cool and become solid within the crust. Sometimes the magma erupts on the surface as lava and creates a volcano.

Around the edges of the Pacific Ocean the large Pacific plate is slowly sliding under other plates it meets. Violent earthquakes and volcanic activity occur in these areas. Scientists describe this part of the world as the Pacific Ring of Fire.

Lava, ash, gas and steam erupt through the crater.

The cone shape of a volcano is built up by ash and lava during several eruptions.

Magma rises from a pool of molten rock called a magma chamber.

The Ring of Fire includes more than half the world's volcanoes. The most dangerous of these volcanoes are ones close to where many people live, such as in Japan, Indonesia and Central America.

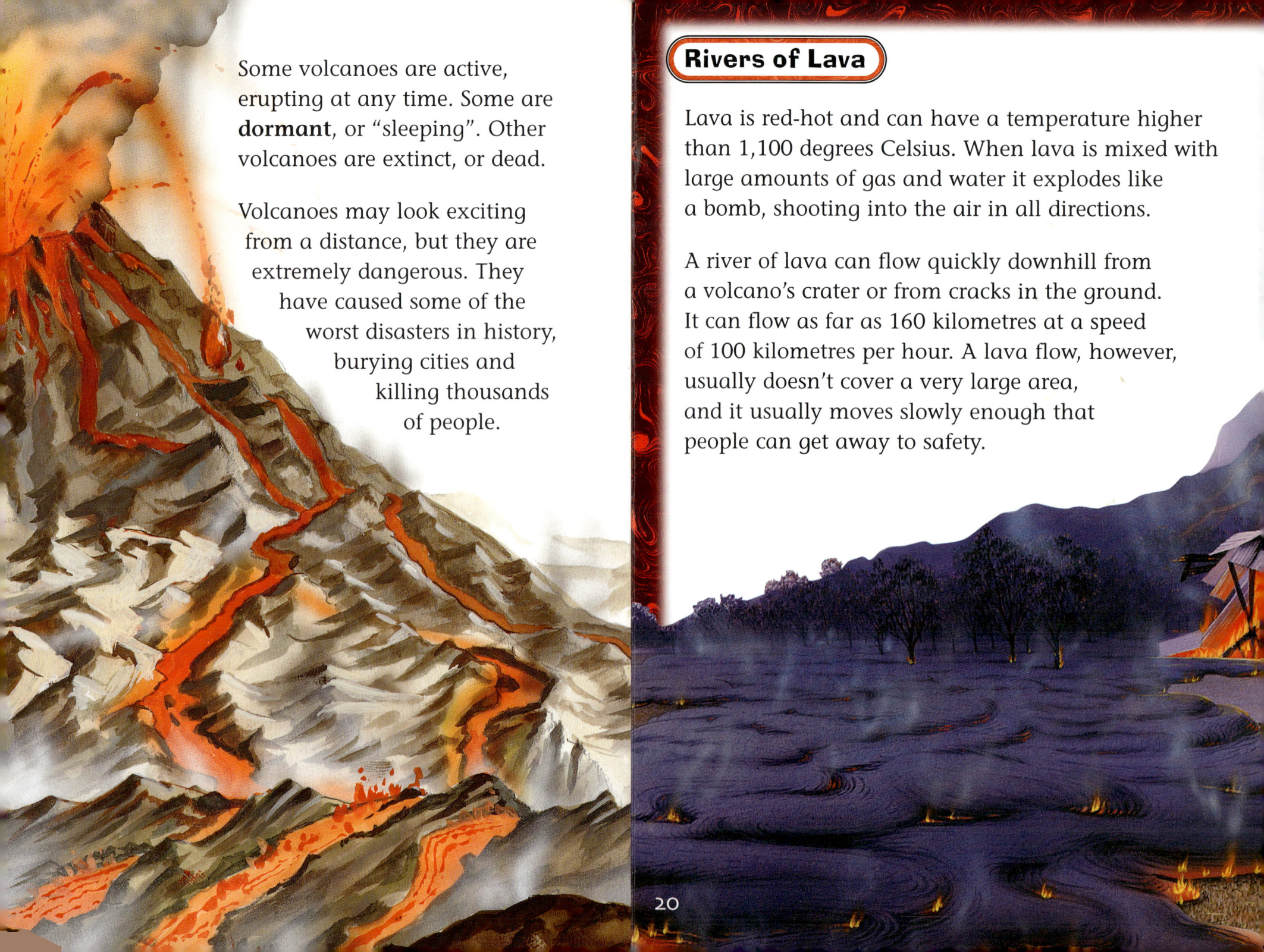

Some volcanoes are active, erupting at any time. Some are **dormant**, or "sleeping". Other volcanoes are extinct, or dead.

Volcanoes may look exciting from a distance, but they are extremely dangerous. They have caused some of the worst disasters in history, burying cities and killing thousands of people.

Rivers of Lava

Lava is red-hot and can have a temperature higher than 1,100 degrees Celsius. When lava is mixed with large amounts of gas and water it explodes like a bomb, shooting into the air in all directions.

A river of lava can flow quickly downhill from a volcano's crater or from cracks in the ground. It can flow as far as 160 kilometres at a speed of 100 kilometres per hour. A lava flow, however, usually doesn't cover a very large area, and it usually moves slowly enough that people can get away to safety.

What a Blast! continued

FAST FACTS

Lava flows can burn buildings and ruin crops. The volcano Kilauea in Hawaii is one of the most active volcanoes on Earth. It has been continually erupting since 1983, destroying more than 180 houses and 12 kilometres of roads.

Gas and Ash

A violent volcanic eruption occurs after a build-up of pressure underground. Gases burst high into the sky, carrying blobs of lava and fine ash. Gas-powered ash clouds can be terrible. The gases can be poisonous and make breathing difficult. Sometimes people need to wear gas masks.

Falling ash can cover vast areas and darken the sky for many days. A small sprinkling of ash adds valuable nutrients to the soil. A build-up of ash, however, can clog roads, ruin roofs, pollute drinking water and destroy farmers' crops.

Volcanic ash and rocks can speed down the side of a volcano. The ash cloud can reach a temperature of 100 degrees Celsius and speeds of up to 250 kilometres per hour.

Daily News   *What a Blast!* continued   Tuesday, November 12, 2002

Ash Chokes City

Yesterday, tonnes of grey ash fell like snow, covering Ecuador's capital city, Quito. The president of the country declared a **state of emergency** and the airport and schools were closed. Many people had difficulty breathing.

The volcano Reventador, 100 kilometres from Quito, erupted without warning last week after lying quietly for 26 years. A cloud of gases and ash shot 14 kilometres into the air.

Hundreds of farmers living near the base of the volcano fled as their once green farms turned into fields of ash.

A Quito resident pedals through a cloud of ash.

After an Eruption

Volcanic eruptions can cause avalanches, or snow slides, and mudflows. Layers of ash can become like thick wet cement when mixed with water from thunderstorms or melted ice. A mudflow can move downhill, gathering speed and burying everything in its path. Sometimes part of a volcano collapses. Within minutes snow and rocks crash at great speed from the top of the volcano to the valleys below.

Eruptions can also start earthquakes and tsunamis. Over a long period of time they can also change the climate. Ash, gas and dust from an eruption can be carried around Earth by strong winds, blocking sunlight and causing long cold winters.

The eruption in 1991 of Mount Pinatubo in the Philippines was one of the largest on record. A cloud of ash spread around Earth.

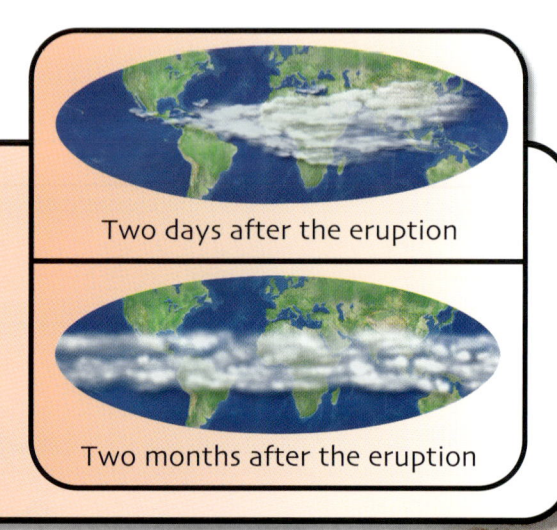

Two days after the eruption

Two months after the eruption

The eruption in 1985 of Nevado del Ruiz in Colombia caused a terrible mudflow that buried the town of Armero, 45 kilometres away.

Keeping Watch

Because volcanoes and earthquakes can be very destructive scientists try to predict when they will occur and how big they will be. Volcanologists study the current activity and the history of volcanoes so they can recognize warning signs that a large eruption may happen.

Volcanologists must be careful when they work close to lava. They work in teams to collect gas and lava samples, and to measure the temperature, the size of craters and the strength of tremors. They wear heat-resistant clothing when they work very close to lava.

Seismologists study earthquakes. They use sensitive machines that can record the tiniest of tremors and the smallest ground movement. The **Richter scale** measures the energy made by an earthquake. Using this scale scientists give earthquakes a **magnitude** rating from 1 to 9. The strongest earthquakes ever recorded measured 8.9 on the Richter scale.

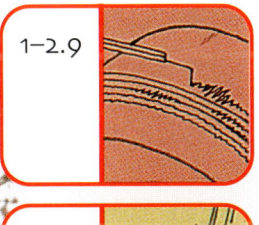

The Richter Scale

Magnitude	Description
1–2.9	Earthquakes of a magnitude up to 2.9 can only be detected by sensitive machines. More than 500,000 occur every year.
3–4.9	At this magnitude lights may swing, but there is little damage. Up to 500,000 such earthquakes occur every year.
5–6.9	Walls can crack and you will definitely feel an earthquake of magnitude 5–6.9. Up to 1,000 of these occur every year.
7–7.9	Buildings collapse and the ground cracks at this magnitude. Between 10 and 20 such earthquakes occur every year.
8–9	Earthquakes of a magnitude 8–9 cause major destruction. Up to 10 occur every year.

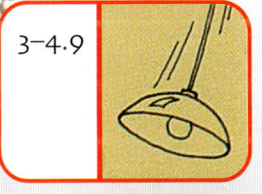

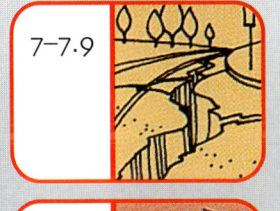

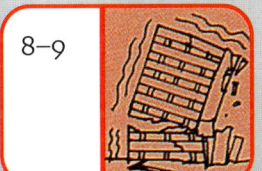

Staying Safe

People who live in earthquake and volcanic areas need to know what to do before, during and after an earthquake or volcano. Homes, offices and schools in earthquake areas can be made safer by attaching heavy furniture to a wall so it doesn't fall over in a quake. During an earthquake people should move away from windows and duck under a doorway, table or bed.

During times of volcanic eruptions it is important that people listen to radio announcements in case they need to **evacuate** the area.

Duck and Cover
Children in earthquake areas such as Japan, California, Vancouver and New Zealand practise earthquake drills at school.

IN FOCUS

Are You Earthquake-Ready?

If you live in an earthquake area make sure you have the following emergency supplies in your home.

Survival Kit

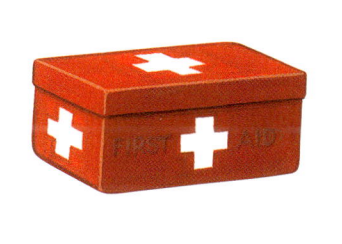

First-aid kit

Torch and whistle

Bottled water, tinned food and a tin opener

Radio and batteries

29

Glossary

convection currents – the movement of heat. Hot rocks rise and cold rocks sink, causing movement of the continental plates.

dormant – a dormant volcano is one that is not active at the present time. A dormant volcano can become active and erupt again.

evacuate – to move away from a dangerous area

fault – a crack in Earth's crust where rocks have shifted

friction – the rubbing of one thing against another

magma – hot liquid rock beneath Earth's surface. When magma escapes to Earth's surface it is called lava.

magnitude – the size, or strength, of an earthquake based on the amount of energy released. The magnitude of an earthquake is measured using the Richter scale.

Richter scale – a scale for measuring the strength of an earthquake. The scale is measured in steps starting at 1. Each step is about 10 times stronger than the one before.

state of emergency – a period of time in which the government stops normal activities in an area because of a disaster or a dangerous situation

subduction – the process of one plate slowly sliding beneath another

tremor – a shaking or trembling movement of Earth's crust. Scientists use portable seismometers to measure tremors.

Index

core	4, 6
crust	4–7, 14, 18
earthquakes	4, 6–12, 18, 24, 26–29
Kobe, Japan	8
Loma Prieta, California	10
earthquake drills	28
faults	10–11
Himalayas	7
mantle	4–7
plates	6–7, 18
San Andreas Fault	10–11
seismologists	27
survival kits	29
tsunamis	12–13, 24
volcanoes	4, 6–7, 12–26, 28
Kilauea, Hawaii	21
Krakatau, Indonesia	13
Mount Pinatubo, Philippines	24
Nevado del Ruiz, Colombia	25
Pacific Ring of Fire	18
Reventador, Ecuador	23
volcanologists	26

Research Starters

1 An active volcano can cause great destruction and loss of life. However, many people live near active volcanoes. Why do you think they choose to live there? Would you want to live near an active volcano?

2 Earth isn't the only planet that has volcanoes and earthquakes. Find out which other planets and moons in our solar system have volcanoes and earthquakes.

3 Earthquakes and volcanoes have occurred in the area of the Mediterranean Sea for more than two million years. Find out about recent volcanic activity and earthquakes in that area.

4 Create your own lava flow! Read books about volcanoes in your library or search the Internet for different ways to make a model volcano.